IMAGES OF ENGLAND

SOUTHWELL

SOUTHWELL: SARACEN'S HEAD HOTEL.

IMAGES OF ENGLAND

SOUTHWELL

DAVID OTTEWELL

TEMPUS

Frontispiece: Saracen's Head Hotel, *c.* 1905. The colourful half-
timbered frontage of the hotel that visitors are more familiar with
today was only restored in 1978. This façade hides a much earlier
building.

First published 2007

Tempus Publishing
Cirencester Road, Chalford,
Stroud, Gloucestershire, GL6 8PE
www.tempus-publishing.com

Tempus Publishing is an imprint of NPI Media Group

British Library Cataloguing in Publication Data.
A catalogue record for this book is available from the British Library.

ISBN 978 0 7524 4438 3

Typesetting and origination by NPI Media Group
Printed in Great Britain

Contents

Acknowledgements

Thanks are due to knowledgeable members of staff in the Local Studies sections of various Nottinghamshire libraries for their help and advice.

Thanks to John and Val Holland.

Although every attempt has been made to contact the relevant copyright holders, the age of the photographs used has, in many cases, made this impossible. If I have inadvertently missed anyone out, I apologise. I will undertake to make amendments in future editions.

Introduction

The small market town of Southwell, lying sixteen miles north-east of Nottingham and six miles west of Newark in Nottinghamshire, would be just like any one of the many hundreds of similar country towns to be found the length and breadth of Britain if it were not for the presence of its magnificent Minster. This building has dominated life in the area for nearly 900 years and makes Southwell of particular interest, giving it a unique character and style.

A survey of the natural resources in the area reveals why a settlement grew up in Southwell; it is situated by the river Greet and within walking distance of the river Trent. In addition, there are a number of smaller natural water sources. Indeed, Southwell takes its name from south-well, as opposed to north-well (Norwell) which is a small village nearby. The pronunciation of the town name however is, even today, hotly disputed. Some call it 'Southwell' while others insist on 'Suth'l'. As well as the presence of abundant water supplies, the area boasts very fertile soil, standing as it does on Keuper Marl, which makes the surrounding district a prosperous farming community.

The first settlers in the area were the Romans, the main Fosse Road being just to the far side of the Trent. There is evidence of a Roman settlement based around a villa situated close to today's Minster School. Later, the settlements of Easthorpe and Westhorpe indicate the presence of Danish invaders and the first church was built in Southwell.

Around AD 956 King Eadwig made a grant of the Manor of Southwell to the Danish Archbishop of York, Oskytel. The Archbishops of York remained lords of the manor for almost 800 years until the privilege passed to the Ecclesiastical Commissioners in 1840.

Southwell is recorded in William the Conqueror's Domesday Book with two manors: one based on the Minster and its surrounds and the other located around the Burgage. In 1108 Thomas II , Archbishop of York, requested the payment of alms by Nottinghamshire parishioners to finance the building of a church in Southwell dedicated to St Mary to act as the main southern outpost of the See. Since then, the Minster and the buildings associated with it have developed over the centuries. Southwell became a favourite retreat for Archbishops of York. They established four deer parks in the area.

The town began to prosper around the Minster. The Saracen's Head, under a different name, is said to date from the fifteenth century when it opened to cater for visitors. Important personages, such as King James VI of Scotland in 1603 on his way to become King of England, passed through. King Charles I took his last ride as a free man from the Saracen's Head in 1646, having already visited the town four years previously with his two sons, on his way to Nottingham to launch the Civil War.

Southwell, despite the presence of the Minster, continued to remain a relative backwater due to its situation away from the main thoroughfares. The Great North Road and the Fosse Way ran six or seven miles away and intersected at Newark, increasing that town's importance and prosperity.

A rural enclave, much of life in Southwell was insular. In the eighteenth century it was one of ten market towns in Nottinghamshire but others, including Newark, Mansfield and Nottingham, were more important and while they thrived, the market at Southwell withered and finally died out only to be revived in the 1970s. Southwell experienced a period of Georgian and Regency splendour, with the building of a number of residences that remain to this day. People were attracted to the town such as the poet Byron, who stayed with his mother on the Burgage between 1804-07.

The arrival of the railways in 1847 helped the development of the town. The Greet Lily Flour Mill opened in the first half of the nineteenth century and, when the House of Correction closed on the Burgage in around 1880, the buildings were developed into a lace factory.

Many would argue that it is the relative backwater that Southwell inhabits that contributes to its charm. Today it attracts many people because of its slower pace of life, its impressive Minster and the fact that a number of the older buildings have survived. It remains an attractive area to live and visit.

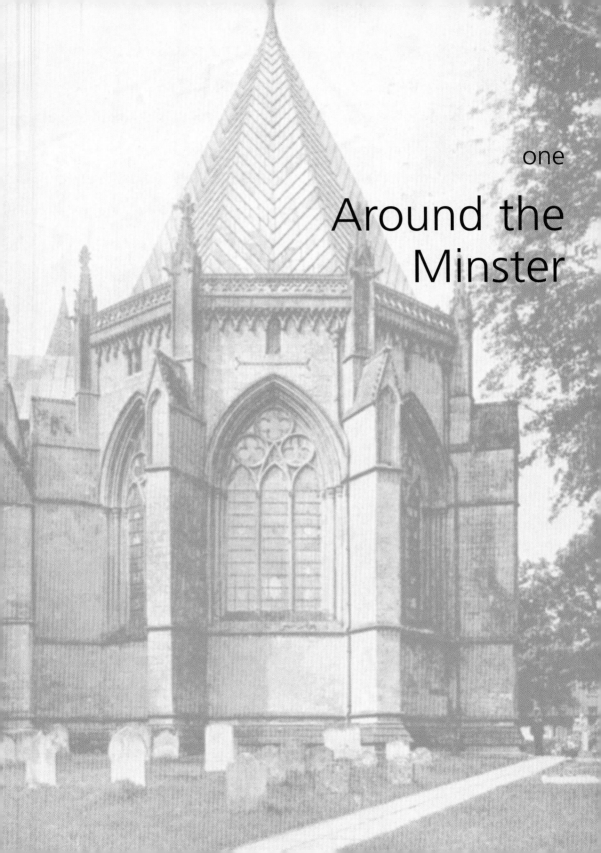

one

Around the Minster

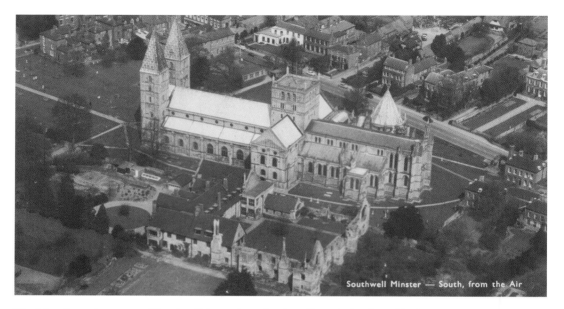

Southwell Minster — South, from the Air

The historic market town of Southwell, located on the river Greet, is dominated by its Minster. Its presence has influenced the development of the town, including the building of many of the properties in adjacent streets.

SOUTHWELL CATHEDRAL FROM N.

Minster from the north, *c.* 1930. King Eadwig granted Southwell to Oskytel, Archbishop of York in around 956. When, in the early twelfth century, the Archbishop of York, Thomas II, had raised money in Nottinghamshire to build St Mary's, he had to begin constructing a new building, for little was already in place.

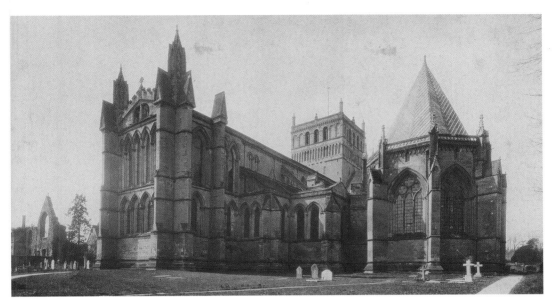

In the thirteenth century, this Norman church was extended and the complete east-end enlarged. In this period of building, the most significant achievement was the Chapter House, begun in 1288.

During the Civil War, parliamentary troops stabled horses in the nave and the Minster only escaped destruction through the actions of Edward Cludd, who lived at Norwood Park. After 1660, restoration work had to be carried out.

Southwell Minster, E.

Left: Lightning struck the spire on the south-west tower of the Minster on 5 November 1711, setting it on fire. The flames spread to the roof of the nave and the central tower destroying the bells, clock and organ. It took seven years for restoration work to be completed.

Below: In 1801 the western spires were removed, the towers strengthened and flat roofs placed on the towers. Another seventy-nine years elapsed before the towers were capped.

Above: The twin western towers are an identifying feature of Southwell Minster. They were crowned with what are referred to locally as 'pepper pots' in the 1880s. Initially, the spires were covered in a herring-bone pattern of slates but, in the 1920s, this was renewed using a rectangular design.

Below: At one time there were a series of elm trees running parallel to Church Street just inside the Minster grounds but, by the Second World War, these had been cleared away leaving an open aspect towards the north side.

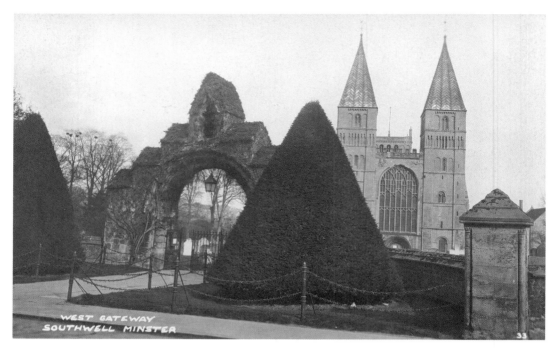

The yew tree has a traditional presence in many churchyards. This pair, flanking the entrance path to the west gateway to the Minster grounds, are believed to date from the middle of the nineteenth century.

The Porta, *c.* 1911. The west gateway, on leaving the Minster grounds into West Gate. On emerging into the road, immediately facing you are three of the Prebendal Houses.

The postcard refers to the house in the foreground as 'Hacketts House' and features the view taken from behind the three Prebendal Houses on West Gate, Dunham, Rampton and Sacrista, towards the west front of the Minster.

A distant view of the Minster from an area known as Harvey's Fields. Around Southwell there are various water sources and a number of narrow waterways. Crossing the foreground is one of these, the Potwell Dyke.

The Archbishop's Palace was developed in the fourteenth and fifteenth centuries on foundations from an even earlier period. A favourite retreat for many archbishops, in 1530, Cardinal Wolsey stayed here during his arguments with Henry VIII. It fell into ruin after the Civil War.

The monument to George Ridding, who was created first Bishop of Southwell on the 1 May 1884 in St Paul's Cathedral. Prior to this, he had been headmaster of Winchester College. The memorial in St Oswold's Chapel in the Minster is a bronze figure by F.W. Pomeroy on a base designed by W.D. Caroe.

An appropriate place to live could not be found in Southwell for the first Bishop so he took up residence in Thurgarton Priory, three miles away. George Ridding was to live there until he died in 1904.

The newly-formed Southwell Diocese covered a large area. To reach his official functions, Bishop Ridding often took the train from Thurgarton station on the Lincoln to Nottingham line. For other journeys, he used a horse and carriage.

The Bishop of Southwell living away from the Minster was not really satisfactory, so architect William D. Caroe was employed to design a home for the Bishop within the Minster complex. The Bishop's Manor saw Bishop Edward Hoskyns take up residence on its completion in 1907.

The Bishop's Manor incorporated parts of the west side of the ruined Archbishop's Palace, being built on the site of the original great hall.

Local photographer Alfred J. Loughton has ascended to the crossing tower of the Minster to take this view. The Vicars Court and Residence is just below the roof line, with Easthorpe stretching into the distance.

Southwell, Vicar's Court.

The Vicars Court is a set of five houses built on the site of the medieval college of Vicars Choral. The main building at the head of the enclave, the Residence dates from about 1689 and is the home of the Provost of Southwell. The other houses were completed in 1780 and a new façade was added to the Residence five years later to bring a unity to the complex.

SOUTHWELL MINSTER FROM VICARS COURT.

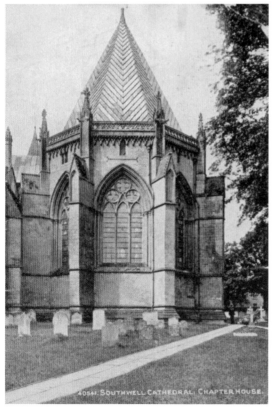

40541. SOUTHWELL CATHEDRAL. CHAPTER HOUSE.

Above: The Residence and Vicars Court, a quiet enclave, slightly detached from life in the town, looks out onto the northern side of the Minster with the Chapter House prominent.

Left: One of the main features of Southwell Minster is the octagonal Chapter House built in the second half of the thirteenth century. It contains thirty-six seats for canons.

Above: The Chapter House is especially noted for its large number of excellent stone carvings featuring leaves, animals, birds etc.

Right: Whilst the identities of the skilled masons who worked on the carvings in the Minster are unknown, this carving of the head of the master mason gives some inkling of the character of the man in charge.

Looking towards the altar. The medieval stained glass in the Minster mostly failed to survive the Civil War period in English history and so, with a few exceptions of imported sixteenth-century and modern glass, the stained glass to be seen today dates from Victorian times.

Some of the panelling and stained glass windows within the Old Palace Hall.

Edward Hoskyns, appointed the second Bishop of Southwell in 1904. Like his predecessor, initially he had to live at Thurgarton Priory until he could take possession of the Bishop's Manor.

Moving with the times, Dr Hoskyns had a motor car, Reg. No. AL 1689, still a rarity in the early years of the twentieth century. A chauffeur was employed to drive him to venues where he performed many of his diocesan duties.

The Bishop of Southwell, Dr Edward Hoskyns, being greeted on the platform of the town railway station on his homecoming, 29 June 1907.

Westgate adorned with flags and banners to welcome home Bishop Hoskyns on 29 June 1907. The Bishop's Manor within the Minster precincts had become the Hoskyns' family home.

The Bishop of Southwell leads a procession of clergy in the grounds of Southwell Minster to celebrate the 800th anniversary of the Minster.

A military funeral being conducted by Bishop Hoskyns. Ninety Southwell men lost their lives as a result of the First World War. A military guard of honour watches as the flag-draped coffin is brought to the graveside.

The Bishop of Southwell at a more personal function – the marriage of his daughter, Phyllis Eleanor, to the Revd Edward Gordon Selwyn, which took place at the cathedral on 4 August 1910.

Funeral - Late Bishop of Southwell Dec 5th 1925.

A solemn occasion at the Minster, with the long procession formed for the funeral service for the Bishop of Southwell on 5 December 1925.

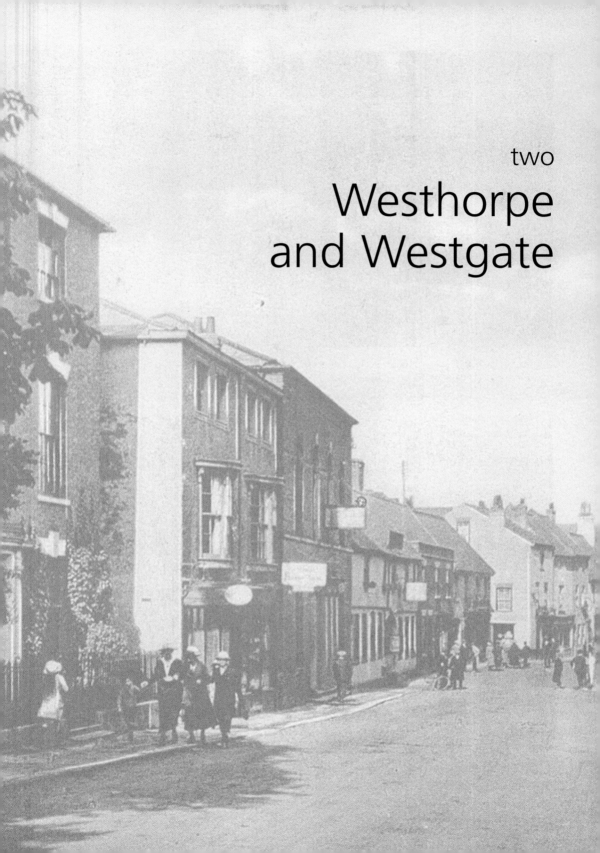

two

Westhorpe
and Westgate

Revd Thomas Coats Cane, Vicar of Thurgarton, built Brackenhurst Hall in 1828. A relation, Henry, born at the hall, became Field Marshall Lord Allenby, First World War leader in the Palestine Campaign.

In 1899, the Hicking family acquired the hall and William Hicking, a Nottingham textile manufacturer, began a series of improvements including adding the lake.

Another of William Hicking's improvements was the development of the rose garden. When he died in 1947, the hall and 260 acres of land were sold to Nottinghamshire County Council.

The Earl of Harrington's hounds at Brackenhurst Hall, *c.* 1910. Like many country estates, the Hickings allowed the hunt to use their land. The presence of the horses is a sign of things to come for today a large equestrian centre is based at Brackenhurst as part of Nottingham Trent University.

Nottingham Farm Institute opened in October 1949 with an initial intake of thirty-four students, all men. The aims were 'training in farm management, farm crafts, farm machinery and the promotion of social and cultural activity'. In 1953 a residential course for women was introduced in 'country house-keeping'. How times have changed!

Descending into Southwell with the town's two churches on the skyline: Holy Trinity to the left and the Minster to the right. The stone to the left was probably for road resurfacing.

The junction of Nottingham Road and Westgate at the very beginning of the 1950s. Note the shop premises on the corner, now long since converted into residential accommodation.

Nottingham Road, once known as Moor Lane, has traditionally provided access between Southwell and Thurgarton. This photograph, dating from 1870, shows the roadway to have been in poor shape at this time. In more recent times, a garage business operated on this corner.

Looking towards Westhorpe, c. 1870. For centuries, Westhorpe was a hamlet on the edge of Southwell, being the centre of framework-knitting in the area. In a survey of 1844, Southwell contained 120 frames, the majority of which were in Westhorpe.

The building of Holy Trinity, Southwell's other church, was prompted by an increase in population. By 1831 there were 3,384 people in the town and the Minster could only accommodate 800. The building was consecrated on 31 March 1846. A total of £2,500 was spent on building work, the most prominent feature of which was the 150ft-tower.

The girls of Southwell Church of England School have assembled, some in fancy dress, to celebrate Empire Day.

Local firm W.D. Tucks of Church Street built the Ideal Cinema on Westgate in 1932 on the site which, up until 1920, had been the home of Marston, Thompson and Evershed Brewery. The cinema complex contained a social club and a dance floor. The shop to the left featured a general store and the one to the right an electrical shop. The cinema could seat 600 with prices from 6d to 1s 6d. It closed in February 1962. Later it was used by Pressac as a base for manufacturing telephones.

Westhorpe Hall, built around 1820, belonged for a long time to the Warrand family. Being of architectural importance today, it is Grade II listed.

Between the wars, Westhorpe Hall became the home of Group Captain Henry Hanmer, well-known in horse-racing circles. After his death in 1984, the hall was sold and today it is divided into apartments.

The Shoulder of Mutton, *c.* 1960. Seen here selling Warwick's Newark Ales, the Shoulder of Mutton was one of many inns within the town. It began around 1780 and continued to trade until 1975, later being converted into a private house.

Even before the recreation ground was designated as such, the land was used for gatherings. In Edwardian times, as here, it was the done thing to stay respectably attired at all times, including wearing a hat, when in public.

Southwell folk lost their lives in both world wars. A war memorial, in traditional style, was erected on the Burgage in 1921. This Memorial Arch, constructed in 1949, provided an ornate entrance at the end of Bishops Drive to the War Memorial Recreation Ground. Previously this had had been land forming part of the Archbishop of York's deer park. The memorial consisted of a row of pillars holding up a stone lintel with a gold inscription. Sadly, less than fifty years after its opening, the concrete had succumbed to water damage.

A hospital fête took place at West Lodge on Westhorpe in 1915. Local photographer Howard Barrett was present with his camera to record this fine collection of nurses.

A postcard by Southwell's other distinguished photographer, Alfred J. Loughton, dating from 1915. The pipes and drums of the Boys' Brigade are passing by the western gate to the Minster along West Gate. They appear to be part of a parade. West Gate, being the location of the main entrance to the Minster grounds, saw many such events.

Opposite above: Although by 1915 the First World War was well underway, the hospital fête at West Lodge seems to have been a jolly affair judging by the fancy dress costumes of a number of the people in the photograph.

Opposite below: The houses and shops to the right back onto the Minster grounds. The house and shop to the left were built across the frontage of the Prebend Oxton II. Much of the Prebend land had been sold in the late eighteenth and early nineteenth centuries. The house was built in 1811 by William Hodgson Barrow. Next to it, and before the shop, is a footpath known as Prebend Passage, dating back to ancient times, which originally crossed the Prebend site.

Southwell.

The Assembly Rooms, *c.* 1910. These were designed and built by Richard Ingleman in 1805. He went on to build the gateway to the House of Correction on the Burgage in 1807 and the Grammar School in 1819. At the time of this picture, the Assembly Rooms look a separate building to the inn next door.

The front of the Saracen's Head has undergone a number of changes over the years. This photograph, dating from the 1950s, shows how one attempt was made to integrate the appearance of the adjacent Assembly Rooms with the inn by painting along in white. Access to the Assembly Rooms from street-level was blocked off and the premises used as extra accommodation by the hotel

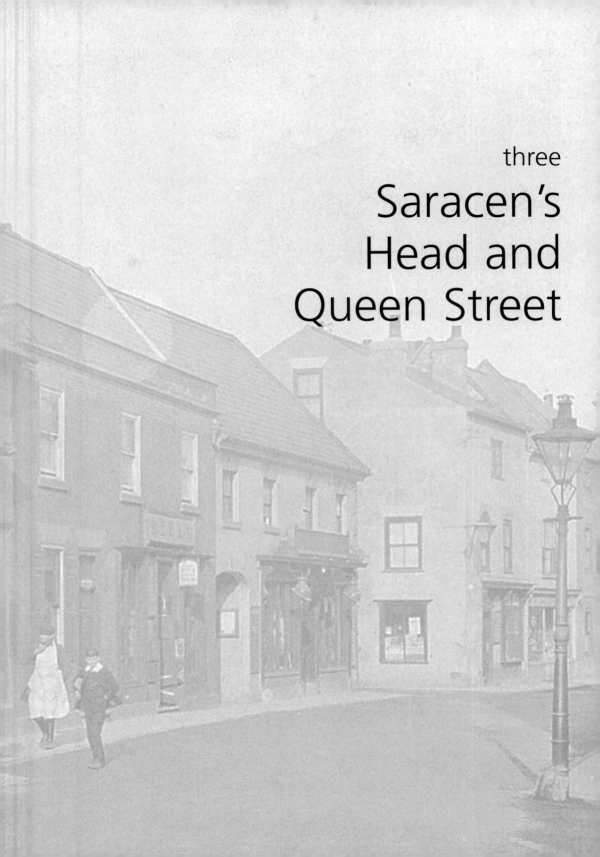

three

Saracen's Head and Queen Street

A faded view of the Saracen's Head in the early years of the twentieth century. A metal sign declares that it acts as the Midland Railway parcel receiving office. Next to the hotel are the premises of Padgetts, who published a number of postcards showing views of the town.

Saracen's Head Hotel, Southwell.—A. Merryfield, Proprietor.

The Saracen's Head offered the service of not only taking and collecting parcels from the railway station; its customers could also be personally conveyed in some comfort to and from the destination.

Saracens Head, Southwell.   1.

The frontage of the Saracen's Head in the 1950s. It is interesting to compare with the previous picture from half a century earlier, as this demonstrates clearly the continual updating of the hotel by different proprietors.

GATEWAY,
YE OLDE SARACEN'S HEAD,
SOUTHWELL, NOTTS.

The wide entrance gates originally offering easier access to the inn's premises for horse-drawn vehicles. The changing times are hinted at by the sign offering the facilities of a garage to house the cars of patrons on this postcard, published soon after 1910.

The courtyard of the Saracen's Head looking out towards Church Street, *c.* 1920. The half-timbered structure to the left dates from the fifteenth century. As the century progressed and more improvements were carried out, the removal of layers of stucco revealed further timbering.

The advert on the rear of this postcard showing the coffee room in the Saracen's Head boasts, 'good old English hospitality with due regard for the comforts as well as the purses of the visitors is still extended by mine hosts'.

During the Civil War, King Charles I arrived at the King's Arms (now the Saracen's Head) on 5 May 1646 to try to negotiate a peace treaty with the Scottish Commissioners based locally. The negotiations proving fruitless, Charles I left the inn on his last journey as a free man, riding to nearby Kelham Hall, where he was taken into custody by the Scottish Army.

Having travelled to Southwell through the night to evade capture, Charles I and his two companions spent the day waiting in this room at the King's Arms while his intermediary, a French diplomat, Jean de Montreuil, held what proved to be abortive negotiations with the Scottish Commissioners based in the Archbishop's Palace.

Links with Charles I are good publicity for the Saracen's Head Hotel. When the King was beheaded by the victorious parliamentary side in 1649, a copy of his death warrant was hung inside the hotel for visitors to see.

The area outside the Saracen's Head is a prominent meeting point in the centre of Southwell. Here the Sutton Lodge of the Nottingham Order of Oddfellows have gathered round their banner. The Lodge was founded in the mid-1800s by a prominent local resident, John Bradwell, manager of Wyldes bank, a farmer and long-time churchwarden of the Minster. He met an unsavoury end when he was knocked down and killed by the Southwell Paddy at Rolleston junction in December 1874.

John R. Starkey, son of Lewis Randle Starkey and owner of Norwood Hall, stood in the 1906 parliamentary election as a Conservative candidate. He is hemmed in by a large attentive crowd on the steps of the Assembly Rooms.

Mr Starkey in the more spacious area in front of the Saracen's Head canvassing in 1906. He defeated Mr Manderville, the Liberal representative by 328 votes.

A group of boys and girls of the Prebend House School posing for the photographer in 1904. The school met in a building situated to the rear of the Saracen's Head.

The Church of England Infants School opened in 1885 on Shepherds Row off Queen Street. Along with Holy Trinity on Westgate, it catered for the educational needs of the younger children in the town.

Another group photograph from the Church of England Infant School. This can be accurately dated to 6 October 1915. Note the little lad holding the blackboard, patriotically dressed in an army cap and jacket. In 1930, the school building fetched £120 when sold to the local WI.

Catholics in Southwell had no permanent place of worship until the church of Our Lady of Victories opened on 12 September 1962. The land on Halam Road, plus £2,000 towards building costs had been bequeathed as early as 1915 by a member of the Shelock family.

In 1908 the town fire brigade, based on Queen Street, consisted of a fire engine and eight men under the control of Robert Ellis, superintendent.

Halam Road with the horse and cart leaving the centre of Southwell. On the left is the junction of the road to the village of Kirklington. Just behind the cart to the left is the Ropewalk. This had originally been known as New Dyke Lane and later Ropemakers Lane. Its name is derived from the occupation of rope making, originally carried out on the western side of the lane.

The present Norwood Hall, built in the 1760s by John Sutton, came into the hands of Lewis Starkey in 1881.

Norwood Park, originally one of the Archbishop of York's deer parks. By the First World War, this estate, owned by the Starkey family, covered 150 acres. Part was requisitioned by the army and troops were housed under canvas.

Estates like Norwood Park not only served as bases to train men ready for the Front but also acted as locations to collect stores and equipment such as wagons and horses. These were then shipped out to France.

Howard Barrett of Southwell produced this postcard of a local recruiting parade in 1915, at a time when there was great need for men to join the forces. It must have been very difficult to resist the call to arms.

One can only wonder how busy the area around Southwell must have been during the First World War with soldiers passing through. Here, A.J. Loughton has captured members of the Royal Engineers with their horses at Southwell in 1915.

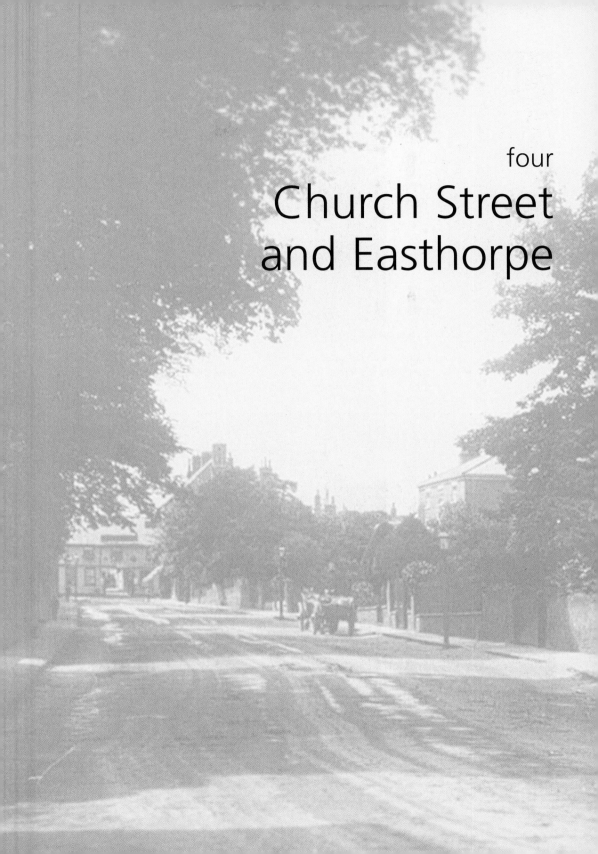

four

Church Street
and Easthorpe

The Crown Hotel, once owned by the Chapter of Southwell Minster, developed into the style of building seen here about 1820 when William Smith became the innkeeper. He developed the property and improved trade so that the Crown rivalled the Saracen's Head as the town's principal inn.

Looking down Church Street from the Saracen's Head. The grammar school designed by Richard Ingleman can be seen to the right. The ornate fencing to the left fronts the grounds of the Nottingham & Notts Bank.

J.H. Kirkby and Sons Ltd had a grocery shop at the top of Church Street from the late Victorian era until the end of the 1950s, when they sold out to the famous Nottingham-based company Burtons. The Kirkbys were a local family, who lived for many years at Hardwick House on Queen Street. J.H. Kirkby used a fleet of delivery carts to supply customers in outlying villages. They were later replaced by vans and lorries.

Boys and masters from Southwell Grammar School line up for the photographer in 1903. The picture was taken next to the school which backed onto the grounds of the Minster.

In Edwardian times, Mr Merryfield, proprietor of the Saracen's Head, used a series of postcards to drum up trade. This one extolled the virtues of the view from the drawing room of his hostelry – of an empty Church Street. You just get a glimpse of the Minster to the right and some large houses to the left. Although a premier area in which to live, this view does not really do it justice.

At one time there were sixteen Prebends in Southwell, i.e. residences for secular canons (Prebendaries) who were members of the Chapter of Southwell Minster. By the end of the eighteenth century, they were no longer needed as homes and were leased out. The Prebend of Palishall was demolished in 1795 and Palishall House built.

After Palishall House was built, there remained a lot of spare land. Another corner fronting Church Street had Willoughby House built on it. Between the two, for many years the land became a builder's yard and more recently a car park, from which a view of Palisall House gardens can be obtained. At one time, this housed part of a tea rooms.

Above: Cranfield House, originally one of the Prebendal Houses, Oxton I, was built by George Mompesson in 1709. This house was later lived in by members of the prominent Southwell family, the Bechers, one of whom, Cranfield Becher, gave his name to the property. Of considerable architectural note, this property appears in Pevsner.

The Hearty Goodfellow – just one of the nineteen inns, taverns and brew houses recorded in the town in the 1832 directory. It was in a cottage in Easthorpe that the famous Bramley apple originated in the early 1800s.

Opposite below: Church Street, *c.* 1910. Originally known as Finkell Street, this thoroughfare runs along the north side of the Minster from the Saracen's Head and subsequently into Easthorpe. It was the site of a number of the Prebendal Houses. To the left is the Vicars Court.

Above: Easthorpe, like its counterpart Westhorpe, was at one time a hamlet and separate from Southwell. Indeed 'thorp' derives from the Danish for hamlet. In the foreground can be seen a gasometer, belonging to Southwell & District Gas Co., founded in 1852. These were situated close to Easthorpe Hall.

Left: Like most communities, Southwell has had a number of football teams over the years. These two gentlemen are brothers H. and W. Bradbury, who played for Southwell St Mary's, formed in 1896. The team later changed its name to Southwell Amateurs.

The crowd gathered for the official opening of the Southwell golf club on 19 October 1911. The nine-hole course had been laid out near Pentalows, the home of the Southwell rugby club. The course proved popular but the military took it over during the Second World War and dug up the ground. After the war it was never relaid and the clubhouse eventually became a house.

The town has been in the centre of a farming area since Roman times. This is a gathering of the Southwell and District Farmers' Club at Hockerton on 5 November 1905. At this date, the annual ploughing match was still within the era of horse power.

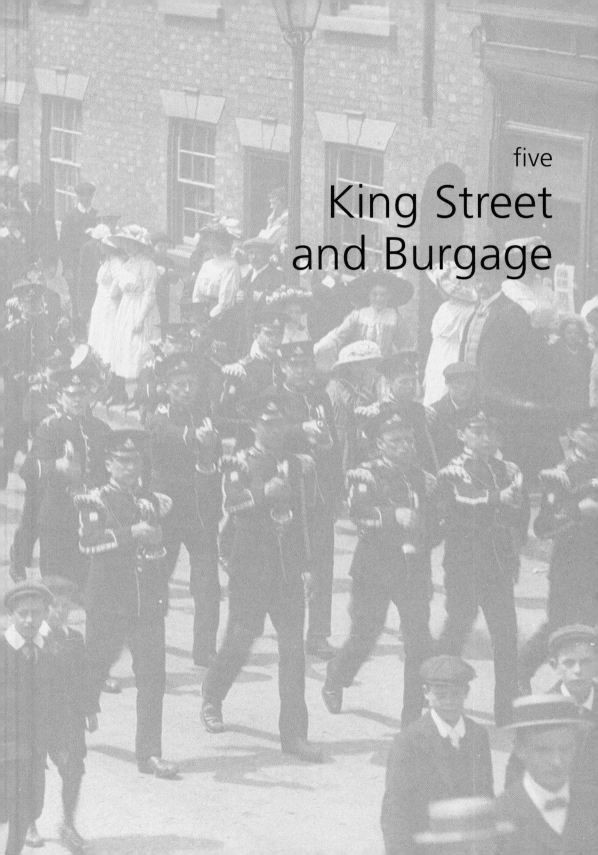

five

King Street
and Burgage

On the corner of Church Street and King Street, the premises of the Union of London and Smiths Bank were once the home of Wyldes Bank, a local company which went bust in 1876, causing financial hardship for a number of people. Later in the twentieth century the National Provincial Bank operated from here.

King Street, the main commercial street in the town. In the 1830s the road was named Farthingate.

The white building, second along from the Saracen's Head, on the corner of King Street and Queen Street and known as Manchester House, was the home of the Loughton family. William Loughton traded as a gentleman's outfitter and hatter. His brother, Alfred John Loughton (1865-1953), also ran his business from here. He is very important to local historians for he took many photographs of the area, a number of which were turned into postcards.

This picture was taken after 1950 when the Georgian house and shop known as Manchester House was demolished to improve vehicular access from King Street to Queen Street. Behind Manchester House stood the Southwell Theatre, which opened in 1816.

King Street in the early years of the twentieth century, with the Admiral Rodney in a prominent position. At this time, Mr and Mrs A. Merryfield were proprietors of both this establishment and the Saracen's Head. Built in the middle of the eighteenth century, the Admiral Rodney took its name from a national hero who, in 1780, led the British fleet that defeated the Spanish at Cape St Vincent.

The Admiral Rodney eventually underwent modernisation as a result of the development of motor transport. The glass covered carriageway entrance at the side of the hotel became incorporated into the building, forming an extension of the main bar.

The Admiral Rodney has changed in appearance since the beginning of the century, as has the type of traffic passing by. The signage indicates the hotel had both AA and RAC approval in the 1960s.

J. Mills and Sons, boot and shoe makers, with their awnings out to protect customers from the sun whilst they browse through the goods on offer.

Howard Barett of Southwell stood with his back to Back Lane when he took this photograph on 23 June 1912. He captured a church parade with band, marching up King Street towards the Burgage. In the background is the Wheatsheaf Inn, which is over 200 years old.

71

The eastern side of King Street with the central stores prominent. The next shop along is Louisa Sheard, milliner.

Built in the last quarter of the eighteenth century, Burgage Manor was owned by the Faulkner family. Between 1803 and 1808, Lord Byron's mother rented the house and during this time the poet spent his vacations from Harrow School and Cambridge there. Byron's room was on the first floor far right.

In later years Burgage Manor experienced a varied history. In addition to being a family home, it has served as a school, convalescent home, youth hostel and as offices for the Darcy Exploration Co., who were exploring in the area for oil.

This photograph of Burgage Manor is not dated but, interestingly, it has a 'for sale' sign in the window over the porch. We know that the Youth Hostels Trust for England and Wales bought the house during the Second World War and operated it a hostel until 1965.

A group of hostellers outside Southwell Youth Hostel. The entrance was to the side of Burgage Manor. The Burgage was the area of grass to the front.

The top of the Burgage was the site chosen for the town war memorial. To the left of the trees can be seen the Grey House. Built in Victorian times, it is unusual for the area in that it is constructed from white bricks as opposed to the mellow red bricks favoured by other properties in the town.

When Bishop Hoskyns blessed the war memorial in 1921, a large crowd gathered to witness the event, headed by the Duke of Portland from Welbeck Abbey and Mr and Mrs John R. Starkey from Norwood Hall.

Even today, the war memorial reminds us of local casualties in the First World War. The Southwell Company of the 8th Sherwood Foresters, commanded by Major John Pickard Becher, left for France in February 1915. Twenty-two men from this company were eventually killed in France. Ninety local men lost their lives in the First World War and twenty-three in the Second World War.

Station Road where it crosses Kirklington Road. The body of Henry Standley was put on display here in 1822. He had murdered a man in Hockerton Moor Wood and had been committed to the house of correction to await his date in court. Before this could happen, he committed suicide. The magistrates ruled that he should be buried at the crossroads as it was believed that, in this grave, his soul would never rest in peace.

From the railway crossing, Station Road rises up across Kirklington Road and onto the Burgage. Much of this section of the town developed in the second half of the nineteenth century with the coming of the railways. Prior to this time it was known as Mill Lane.

The Midland Railway arrived as a single track from the main line at Rolleston in 1847. The station buildings were erected in 1860. A single line was built to Mansfield in 1871 which operated a passenger service until 1929. The Southwell to Rolleston 'Paddy' service continued to operate until 1959, when a single ticket was priced at an uneconomic 6d.

Built in 1861-3, the Newcastle Arms initially took the name 'the New Inn' but was renamed after the Dukes of Newcastle, whose ancestral home, Clumber House, was nearby. The wagons drawn up outside the inn are loaded with coal from the coal yard at the station.

Opposite above: Railway employees surveying the damage at an accident in Southwell station on 25 June 1907. In the background Cauldwell's Flour Mill can be seen.

Opposite below: Charles Cauldwell bought the flour mill from the Booth family in 1851. Unfortunately it suffered major fire damage in 1867 and 1893. After the second fire, insurance money helped restore the mill and a 76ft tower was incorporated. Into this, a 6,000-gallon water tank was fitted and linked to an automatic sprinkler system. This turned out to be an inspired move, as it limited damage when fire broke out again in 1917.

RAILWAY SMASH AT SOUTHWELL.
JUNE 25TH 1907.

An advertising postcard for Cauldwell's Flour Mill, showing its idyllic setting on the river Greet. The card proudly promotes 'Greet Lily Flour' as the winner of the Nottinghamshire Baker's Cup for three consecutive years from 1907-9. The company went on to win the cup in two further years before the First World War, in 1912 and 1914.

Normanton Hall dates back to the 1860s when it was built by the Burrows family, who had been the founders of the Staverley Iron and Coal Co. They were still the owners when Howard Barrett recorded this energetic scene prior to the First World War.

six

Rolleston and Fiskerton

Above: An aerial view of Rolleston parish church, *c.* 1950. This village, 3 miles east, south-east of Southwell, is bounded on the south and the east by the river Trent and intersected by the river Greet.

Left: Village Cross. There is some conjecture as to the original purpose of the cross. The standard work on the subject, A. Stapleton's *Notes on the Crosses of Nottinghamshire, Past and Present* (1903), enthuses, 'we believe Rolleston is the only village in the county possessing at the present time the remains of not less than three ancient crosses'. However, the author was unsure of their origins.

Above: Kate Greenaway (1846–1901), the Victorian children's author and illustrator first visited relatives in Rolleston in 1847. Although she spent her adult life in London, she often visited Rolleston in her childhood and these experiences profoundly influenced her later work.

Below: Mention is made of a mill at Rolleston in the Domesday Book. This building, known as Rolleston watermill and powered by the waters of the river Greet, had various millers over the years. Between the wars, it eventually came into the hands of the Longden family, owners of Fiskerton Mill, who worked it up until the Second World War.

Although a quiet backwater, Rolleston began to attract crowds from 1898 when the Southwell Hunt Race Course Company Ltd was formed. The group leased land from John Manners Sutton next to the station in Rolleston. In 1908 they ran three National Hunt horse-race meetings. By 1912 this had increased to four per year.

First mentioned as an inn in 1832, the most unusual feature of the Crown Inn is the Wishing Tree standing in the forecourt. People, especially lovers, would travel long distances so they could have the opportunity to climb through the gap in the trunk and make a wish.

Rolleston in 1918. The following year, the village saw an influx of people when the Ministry of Agriculture and Fisheries formed a farm settlement on nearly 3,000 acres, some of it in Rolleston parish, to help resettle soldiers returning from the First World War.

Fiskerton station on the Midland Railway line. It was built unusually close to the next station on the line, for Rolleston station, linking to Southwell. is less than a mile away.

Fiskerton Mill dates from the mid-eighteenth century. Formally a lace thread factory, it was converted to corn milling in 1837. In 1851 a fire destroyed the front and killed five men. After repair, it continued making flour until the 1920s, before switching production to animal feed. This continued up until the 1980s.

A 1969 account reports that two reservoirs once served Fiskerton Mill, but that one had recently been filled in with ash from Staythorpe Power Station. The mill had been converted to electrical power in 1963.

Large houses by the river Trent were something of a status symbol. In 1861 there were only seventy-seven homes in the village, but few were of the size seen here. The population in 1901 numbered 369.

In this riverside village, a number of the residents would make their living from the Trent and the Greet. There were a number of wharves where boats could tie up, although this photograph, possibly from prior to the Second World War, suggests a somewhat neglected state.

The appropriately named 'Trent House' by the river in 1921. Barges plying their trade up and down would, at one time, have found this a convenient and safe place to stop.

Above: The Bromley Arms took its name from Lord Bromley of East Stoke Hall, who often crossed over the Trent to go hunting. Indeed, this is a popular crossing point with a ferry traditionally operating on the river. During the Wars of the Roses, soldiers crossed here to participate in the Battle of East Stoke.

Opposite below: Making a pontoon bridge across the Trent appears to have been a popular task set by troop trainers during the early years of the First World War judging by the number of postcards that have survived depicting this activity.

Above: During the First World War, Fiskerton Camp was just one of many 'canvas' camps around the country preparing recruits for the rigours they would face in the trenches once they were shipped to France.

Red-bricked St Denis church in Morton, erected in 1756, has two bells in its embattled tower. After viewing the church, Pevsner commented, 'charming from outside, disappointing within'.

Morton Grange on the edge of Fiskerton. No explanation can be found for the presence of the tent in the grounds.

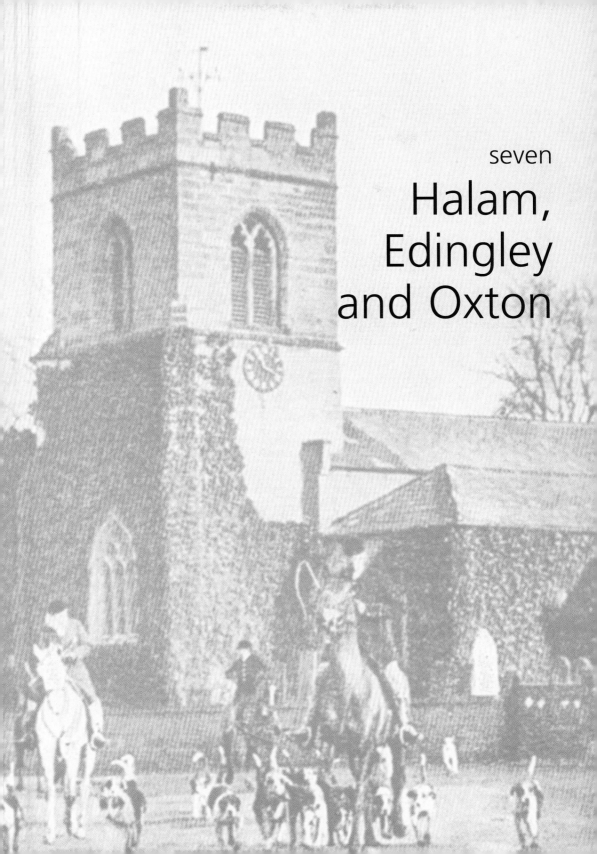

seven

Halam, Edingley and Oxton

Manor House, Halam, c. 1930. In late Victorian times, until his death in 1910, Lewis Randle Starkey and his family at Norwood Hall profoundly influenced life in Halam, building the school and school house, converting a cottage into a reading room and being leading lights in the building of the Vicarage in 1910. They also provided many treats for the villagers.

St Michaels, Halam is an ancient church with features dating from Norman times. Restored in 1884-9 at a cost of £1,600, it has seating for 130. Interesting to note are four windows in the nave which were designed by Burne Jones and added in 1919.

On the main route from Mansfield to Southwell, Halam had two coaching inns almost next to each other at the bottom of steep Halam Hill. Once a farmhouse, the Plough finally closed in 1992 and is now a family home.

The Waggon and Horses is believed to have been built in 1752, just prior to the turnpike road being established in 1759. It provided stables and a smithy for travellers at the rear. The village shop was eventually incorporated into the pub in the 1980s.

In the early years of the twentieth century, Halam was very much a farming community. In 1901 the vast majority of the 255 inhabitants earned their living from farming or related trades. Apple growing thrived in the area until the 1920s when prices dropped due to foreign competition.

The Wesleyan Chapel in Halam cost £368 to build in 1896. Dwindling attendances meant it being re-designated as the village hall in 1989.

Arthur Mee in his book, *King's England*, regarded Edingley (3 miles west, north, west of Southwell) as a 'trim little place… abounding in orchards'. Today, it is still very much a rural backwater.

St Giles, Edingley with its unusual two-bell tower. The church was restored under the care of the architect Mr Hodgson Fowler.

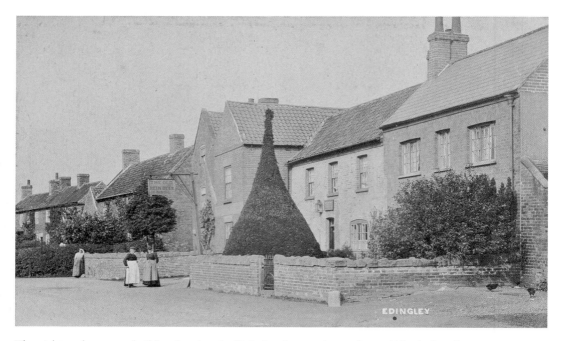

The eighteenth-century building housing the Reindeer Inn survives today on Edingley's main street. The scene differs in the present without the unusually-shaped tree, now sadly no more, and the farthest section of the inn, beyond the sign, which has been demolished.

The Wesleyan Chapel at Edingley opened in 1838. The porch was added in 1893 when the building was re-seated. The sender of the postcard remarks that, 'I went to this chapel on Sunday night, there were about a dozen there'. With seating for 100, this must have meant the building felt quite empty!

The Railway Tavern with William Pearson as landlord did not last long in Edingley. He appears in the 1912 directory as a shopkeeper and beer retailer but has disappeared four years later. The low cottage to the side has now been demolished.

Edingley post office, *c.* 1910. At this period, letters arrived in the village at 6.45 a.m. from Southwell and were then delivered around the area. A second delivery arrived late afternoon and could be collected from the post office. Post was despatched from here twice daily.

St Peter and St Paul in Oxton has parts dating from the Norman period. The Sherbrooke family supervised restoration in 1898, at a cost of £1,300. There are various mementos relating to the family and their exploits to be found in the church.

The Sherbrooke family were associated with Oxton from the sixteenth century. Originally a manor house stood on the estate. This was demolished and a hall built. Henry Porter Sherbrooke (1810–87) enlarged the hall which, unfortunately, was demolished in the 1950s.

Part of Henry Porter Sherbrooke's improvements to the Oxton Estate included the damming of a stream (a tributary of the Dover Beck) to form an ornamental lake as a centrepiece to the 200-acre estate.

Lord Harrington's hounds passing in front of St Peter and St Paul, Oxton. There were a number of horse-riding people within the village in Edwardian times.

The Green Dragon, *c.* 1910. Until the 1920s, the Green Dragon Inn also served as a dairy farm. It was not unusual at this time for a building to have dual uses or for people to carry out multiple roles in small communities. In 1912, the landlord is listed as John Marriott Morley.

The Green Dragon seen in the 1920s. Although this postcard was purchased in Oxton as late as 1972, the writer notes that the wing of the inn in front had been rebuilt. In fact, Nottingham Cooperative Society had bought the pub in 1953 and demolished the remaining farm buildings to form a car park for patrons.

Oxton in the early 1920s. James Spendlove served as the village sub postmaster at this time and letters were received through the nearest town, Southwell.

The other hostelry in Oxton in the early years of the twentieth century was the Bridge Inn.

Oxton (5 miles south-west from Southwell) had a population of 455 in 1901, but this had declined to 405 by the 1911 census. The majority of the adult population were engaged in agriculture.

New Road, Oxton. The poor road surface means that this thoroughfare does not really live up to its name. No wonder that motorists were often looking under their bonnets in the 1920s when having to contend with such conditions.

Oxton School had been endowed by M. Sherbrooke in 1783. It was rebuilt and reopened on 14 November 1870. By the start of the First World War, Harry Hodgkinson held the post of master and his wife, Mrs Florence Hodgkinson, that of infants mistress. In 1916 there were fifty-eight boys and girls on the register and fifty-two infants.

In June 1914, King George V and Queen Mary paid a visit to the area. They had many scheduled visits, including one to Mansfield on 24 June. Crowds, such as this one at Oxton, gathered on the route the royal cavalcade would take to catch a glimpse of the monarch in the pre-television era.

eight

Farnsfield

A motor accident outside the old White Post Inn at Farnsfield on 19 August 1912. The white post was a traditional sign to show the availability of food, accommodation and stabling for travellers.

In 1926 the owners, Chesterfield Brewery, demolished the old White Post Inn, seen above, and constructed this new building on a plot behind the old one.

At one time, Farnsfield Mill also went by the name of 'Straws Mill'. It stood on a ridge facing Mansfield Road.

In the days before widespread private ownership of cars, people in villages had to rely on walking, bicycles or other locals with horse-drawn vehicles. In Farnsfield, for a number of years, Mr Robinson provided such a service with a horse and carriage which he also used to make deliveries.

Farnsfield Village Green in the early 1920s. It is said that, at one time, a maypole stood here. The shop beyond the green is a saddler's and a horse's harness can be seen hanging outside.

The same view thirty years later. A petrol pump now appears on the green demonstrating the progress of transport in the twentieth century. Some may remember a time when there also used to be a bus shelter there. The van in the foreground is of a style now long disappeared.

The Red Lion appears in the 1832 directory. Early licensees saw some extremes of fortune. For instance, in 1874 the premises caught fire three nights running! In 1883 Mansfield Brewery bought the inn.

Today, with almost universal ownership of at least one telephone, it is difficult to imagine a time when most people had to go out to make a call. Here, in the early 1950s, the shop opposite the Red Lion offers customers the opportunity to 'telephone from here'.

Above: A fire destroyed most of the village church in Farnsfield and so, architects Hines and Evans designed a new one incorporating what remained of the old one – just a bit of the tower. The project cost £2,760 and opened in 1860 with a dedication by the Bishop of Lincoln.

Left: Farnsfield war memorial was unveiled in the grounds of the parish church on 27 August 1922.

The Vicarage in 1920 when Canon McKee, Vicar of Farnsfield, lived there.

Mrs Evelyn P. Pidock served as sub postmistress in this building for thirty-four years until 1946 when the post office was transferred to Main Street.

The hall began life less grandly as a farmhouse but was extended in the mid-eighteenth century by John Watson. The stucco-effect was a later addition. In the first quarter of the twentieth century (from when this picture dates), John Harwood Cash lived here and, later, the Linney family.

The drive to the hall from Blidworth Lane with the lodge just through the entrance. Information supplied suggests that the gentleman on the horse was the groom at the hall.

Main Street at the beginning of the First World War. How times have changed, for it is doubtful today that a photographer could find space between parked cars, or time between constantly passing vehicles, to pose children in the road to take a photograph.

From Victorian times through the first half of the twentieth century, Farnsfield had five public houses. One of these was the New Inn, shown here on the left. For much of this time, it belonged to the Tipping family. The New Inn, demolished in 1960, became the site of the Warwick Arms.

Main Street has featured a number of different shops over the years. The one with the prominent 'Hovis' sign was Hutchinson's bread shop.

Looking down Main Street from the opposite direction with the New Inn in the distance, *c.* 1905.

The distinctive Cooperative Stores frontage can be seen to the extreme right-hand side of this 1950s picture of Main Street. Also visible are some of the other small shops typical of a large village at this time.

The Plough Inn dates from at least the seventeenth century but underwent extensive alterations in the 1740s.

The Plough Inn from the other direction, seen here selling Mansfield Ales. Along beyond the pub are a set of properties that have now disappeared to allow road access.

The Grange stood at the Southwell Road end of the village. At one time it was the home of the Miss Whitakers. Later, between the wars, it was owned by Alex Straw J.P.

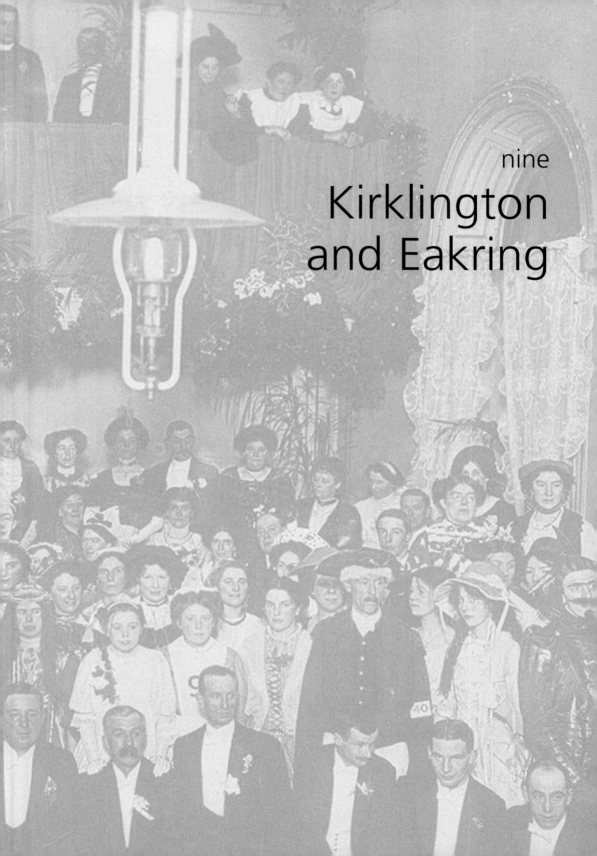

nine

Kirklington
and Eakring

Kirklington Hall was built towards the end of the eighteenth century on earlier foundations. By 1853 Earl Manvers owned the hall. A later owner, the railway magnate Thomas Craven, modernised the building, creating the present structure in 1904.

During the twentieth century, the army took possession of the hall and later BP, who had oil wells in the area, had offices in part of the building. In 1957 the Rodney School, originally founded in the Admiral Rodney Hotel in Southwell in 1945, moved to Kirklington Hall.

On 19 December 1912, locals turned out in force to support a fancy dress ball in aid of the organ fund of St Swithin's church, Kirklington. Southwell photographer Howard Barrett took the picture but there is no indication of where the event took place.

St Andrew's church, Eakring. Parts of the tower date from the thirteenth and fourteenth centuries. Within the tower there are three bells. The church was restored in 1881. The clock, fitted to celebrate Queen Victoria's Golden Jubilee, was restored in 2006.

The Revd Cator set in progress the building of Eakring Rectory. Mr J.G. Finch Noyes of London was engaged as architect and Smith and Lunn of Newark completed the construction in Queen Anne style, using red bricks with white dressing at a cost of £21,000. It was formally opened in October 1886 after the Harvest Festival Service.

The Cator Hall, standing adjacent to St Andrew's church, was built in 1923 with money left by the former vicar, Revd William Lumley Bertie Cator, who served the parish for over thirty years. It was officially opened in 1924. The old church gates are a feature now sadly gone.

An Eakring bride, Elsie Smith, in the rectory gardens before her marriage to Arthur Hemphrey.

Kirklington Road, Eakring, seen from the corner by the Wesleyan Methodist Chapel. The white gateposts to the left lead to Old Church Farmhouse. Beyond are Albemarle Cottages and then March Cottages, after which can just be seen the roof of another cottage which was later demolished and is now the site of the Cator Hall.

Kirklington Road with the Victorian-built Lanes Farm to the left. Further along are the Village Stores. This has been a village shop since the 1850s. Prior to this, one of Eakring's many alehouses, The Fox, operated from the site.

Triumph Road, a small enclave of properties built by Southwell Rural District Council just after the Second World War. The white-washed building in the centre of the picture is the village shop, which was extended and turned into a cooperative after 1945.

Main Street, Eakring, once known as Town Street, seen here from the junction with Kirklington Road. Note the white painted telephone box.

Looking down Wellow Road. For many years this was called Tork Lane. The steps lead to an entrance to the Savile Arms. Chestnut Farm can be seen on the right-hand side.

The Queen's Head public house on Wellow Road (Tork Lane) with C. Marshall as licensee. It remained as a pub until 1961 and continued to sell petrol for ten years after that.

Bilsthorpe Road entering Eakring just beyond Apple Cottage, shown on this postcard dating from the 1950s.

The first building seen on entering Eakring from Bilsthorpe is Apple Cottage. Writing on the back of this postcard suggests that the lady in the doorway may be Harriet Rayworth and the farmer holding the horse, Mr Key.

The foundation stone of the village school was laid by Mr and Mrs Henry Savile of Rufford Abbey, 23 March 1877. A total of £1,053 was spent on the project. Pupil numbers declined after the Second World War and the school finally closed in December 1964. The last teachers were Mrs J. Rushby and Mrs G. Bates.

Main Street with Ryalls Farm to the right. After Church Lane, and running parallel to it, is Ryalls Cottage. Greenfield Row, built in 1841, fronts Main Street. Beyond can be seen a white portion of Walnut Cottage. In the 1940s, Mr and Mrs Burne lived here and ran a small grocer's shop.

Church Lane, *c.* 1950. Chapel House, to the right, began life in 1837 as a Primitive Methodist Chapel. After becoming redundant in the 1930s, it was converted to residential use. The semi-detached houses a little further down were built in the 1940s for agricultural workers.

The D'Arcy Exploration Co. found oil in Eakring in June 1939. This proved extremely useful during the Second World War. In March 1943, forty-two American Roughnecks arrived in the area and helped the British extract 100,000 tons of oil in a year. The 'nodding donkey' became a familiar sight around Eakring.

Holding tanks at Eakring. Oil production at Eakring reached its peak during the war years, but the activities of British Petroleum continued in the village until 1969.

Other local titles published by Tempus

Haunted Nottingham

ANDREW WRIGHT

The streets and buildings of Nottingham, it seems, are alive with the undead: ghosts, ghouls and things that go bump in the night. *Haunted Nottingham* explores the supernatural side of the city and its surrounding areas, featuring chilling reports of unexplained happenings and ghostly apparitions – accumulated by ghost-hunter author, Andrew Wright over more than 30 years' paranormal research.

978 07524 4194 8

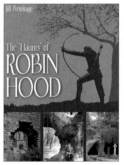

The 'Haunts' of Robin Hood

JILL ARMITAGE

In the distant past, Sherwood Forest was a vast woodland – impenetrable and uncharted. In this dark realm grew the legend of Robin Hood. But does the outlaw hero still linger around the same sites mentioned in the old ballads? Through hidden caves, ancient abbeys and shadowed forests, this volume searches for the ghosts of the past and will fascinate anyone with an interest in the rich folklore of Nottinghamshire.

978 07524 4331 7

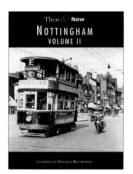

Nottingham Then and Now Volume Two

DOUGLAS WHITWORTH

With a mixture of contemporary and vintage images of Nottingham, this book takes a nostalgic look at the buildings at the very heart of the city and how they used to be, contrasting each one of them with a modern-day equivalent. Providing a fascinating record of the changing cityscape, this book will appeal to anyone who's ever lived and worked in the city, at any time in its rich and varied history.

978 07524 3100 0

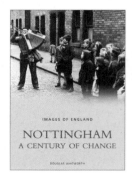

Nottingham: a Century of Change

DOUGLAS WHITWORTH

This fascinating collection of more than 180 old photographs traces some of the many exciting changes seen in Nottingham over the last century. All aspects of life in Nottingham as it used to be are recorded here, including the buildings and the individuals that characterised the city.

978 07524 0767 8

If you are interested in purchasing other books published by Tempus, or in case you have difficulty finding any Tempus books in your local bookshop, you can also place orders directly through our website

www.tempus-publishing.com